PAUL GAYLER

Vegetables

Photography by SIMON WHEELER

THE MASTER CHEFS
WEIDENFELD & NICOLSON
LONDON

PAUL GAYLER was one of the first chefs in Britain to craft truly innovative dishes for vegetarians, for which he built an enviable reputation while he was head chef at Inigo Jones in Covent Garden.

After 23 years dedicated to the kitchens of some of the most respected restaurants in London, he is now executive chef at The Lanesborough Hotel at Hyde Park Corner. His cooking for The Conservatory restaurant there combines classical disciplines with Oriental overtones.

His first book, *Virtually Vegetarian*, was published in 1995 and his second, *Great Value Gourmet*, in 1996. He has appeared on HTV's *Green Grow the Dishes* series and also on BBC-TV's *Hot Chefs*. He lives in Leigh-on-Sea with his wife and four children.

Photograph by Ben Johnson

CONTENTS

The love of vegetables is the

root of all good cooking.

INTRODUCTION

As more and more exotic vegetables are finding their way into our shops, and such specialities as chicory, pumpkin and artichokes are joining the familiar carrots, onions and cabbage in our supermarkets, there are new tastes and textures to experience and new techniques of cooking and flavouring to learn. Thankfully, the days of badly prepared and overcooked vegetables are long gone. We now place far more importance on them as a vital component of a successful meal, recognizing that they provide not only essential vitamins and minerals, but also colour, texture and varied flavours.

The time is ripe to restore vegetables to their rightful place as an interesting addition to the plate or as a course in their own right. I have put together ten of my favourite recipes, which are easy to follow and demonstrate the versatility of vegetables. I hope you will enjoy them. Bon appétit!

Paul

GADO GADO

125 G/4 OZ NEW POTATOES

2 CARROTS, CUT INTO
  MATCHSTICKS

125 G/4 OZ FRENCH BEANS

85 G/3 OZ CUCUMBER, CUT INTO
  MATCHSTICKS

50 G/2 OZ BEANSPROUTS

2 TABLESPOONS VEGETABLE OIL

275 G/10 OZ FIRM TOFU, CUT INTO
  1 CM/½ INCH SLICES

SALT AND FRESHLY GROUND BLACK
  PEPPER

½ A CHINESE CABBAGE OR ICEBERG
  LETTUCE, LEAVES SEPARATED

8 QUAILS' EGGS, HARD-BOILED AND
  HALVED

PEANUT SAUCE

6 TABLESPOONS SESAME OIL

1 FRESH RED CHILLI, SEEDED AND
  CHOPPED

125 G/4 OZ CRUNCHY PEANUT
  BUTTER

6 TABLESPOONS VEGETABLE STOCK

1 GARLIC CLOVE, CRUSHED

1 TABLESPOON SOY SAUCE

2 TABLESPOONS SUGAR

JUICE OF 1 LEMON

SERVES 4

Boil the potatoes until tender. Drain, then peel them while they are still hot, slice and keep warm.

Cook the carrots and beans separately in boiling salted water, retaining their crispness. Drain them and add to the potatoes; keep warm. Add the cucumber and beansprouts to the vegetables.

Heat the oil in a frying pan and fry the tofu slices until golden. Season and drain on paper towels.

For the sauce, heat 3 tablespoons of the sesame oil in a small saucepan and fry the chilli until soft. In another pan, heat the peanut butter, add the stock and boil for 2 minutes. Add the chilli and its oil and remove from the heat, then add the garlic, soy sauce, the remaining sesame oil and the sugar. Season to taste and add the lemon juice; the dressing may separate slightly.

To serve, season the warm vegetables. Arrange the Chinese cabbage or lettuce leaves on the serving plates. Top with the tofu, the warm vegetables and the quails' eggs. Coat lightly with the sauce.

PAN-FRIED POTATO TERRINE
with dried fruits

25 G/1 OZ SMOKED BACON, FINELY
   DICED
½ ONION, FINELY CHOPPED
675 G/1½ LB WAXY POTATOES
SALT AND FRESHLY GROUND BLACK
   PEPPER
125 G/4 OZ MIXED DRIED FRUITS
   (PRUNE, APPLE, APRICOT), CUT
   INTO 1 CM/½ INCH DICE
2 EGGS
85 ML/3 FL OZ DOUBLE CREAM
25 G/1 OZ GRUYÈRE CHEESE,
   GRATED
GRATED NUTMEG
25 G/1 OZ BUTTER

SERVES 8–10

Begin making the terrine a day or
two before you want to serve it.
Preheat the oven to 180°C/350°F/
Gas Mark 4.

Heat a frying pan until hot, add
the bacon and sauté over a high
heat to release its fat, add the
onion and sauté together until
lightly golden. Leave to cool.

Grate the potatoes coarsely and
place in a bowl. Add the bacon
and onion and season lightly. Add
the dried fruits, eggs, cream and
cheese and mix well. Season again
with salt, pepper and nutmeg.

Line a 900 g/2 lb loaf tin with
clingfilm. Pack the tin with the
potato mixture and place in the
oven to cook for up to 3 hours,
until tender when tested with a
skewer. Leave to cool completely.

To serve, cut the terrine into
1–2 cm/½–¾ inch thick slices and
fry in the butter until golden and
slightly crisp. Serve hot.

VEGETABLE FRITTERS
in Indian spiced batter

1 AUBERGINE, SLICED INTO 1 CM/
 ½ INCH CUBES

8 CAULIFLOWER FLORETS

2 COURGETTES, THICKLY SLICED

125 G/4 OZ FRENCH BEANS,
 BLANCHED AND DRAINED

VEGETABLE OIL FOR DEEP-FRYING

SALT

SPICY BATTER

175 G/6 OZ CHICKPEA FLOUR

½ TEASPOON BAKING POWDER

1 TEASPOON CORNFLOUR

½ TABLESPOON EACH OF GROUND
 CUMIN, CORIANDER, MILD
 CURRY POWDER AND TURMERIC

CHUTNEY MAYONNAISE

1 TABLESPOON MANGO CHUTNEY,
 CHOPPED

125 ML/4 FL OZ MAYONNAISE

1 TABLESPOON GRATED FRESH
 GINGER

SERVES 4

Place all the batter ingredients in a large bowl, mix well, then stir in enough water to form a light batter. Place all the vegetables in the batter, stir well to coat and leave for 30 minutes.

Make the chutney mayonnaise by mixing all the ingredients together in a small bowl. Chill.

Heat the oil to 180°C/350°F or until a cube of bread browns in 30 seconds. Drop tablespoons of the vegetables in batter, one by one, into the hot oil and fry until golden and crisp. Drain on paper towels and season lightly with a little salt.

When all the vegetable fritters are cooked, serve hot, accompanied by chutney mayonnaise or your favourite dip or sauce.

MAPLE-GLAZED PUMPKIN TATIN
with sweet spices

25 G/1 OZ BUTTER

450 G/1 LB PUMPKIN FLESH

2 TABLESPOONS MAPLE SYRUP

2 TABLESPOONS SHERRY VINEGAR
    OR RED WINE VINEGAR

15 G/½ OZ FRESH GINGER, FINELY
    CHOPPED

1 TEASPOON GROUND CINNAMON

½ TEASPOON GROUND CUMIN

250 G/9 OZ PUFF PASTRY, THAWED
    IF FROZEN

1 EGG YOLK, BEATEN WITH
    1 TABLESPOON WATER, TO GLAZE

SERVES 6–8

Preheat the oven to 200°C/400°F/ Gas Mark 6. Smear the butter over the base of a 22 cm/9 inch cast-iron frying pan with an ovenproof handle or a flameproof cake tin.

Cut the pumpkin into wedges, 1 cm/½ inch thick. Mix the maple syrup with the vinegar, ginger, cinnamon and cumin and pour into the buttered pan. Arrange the pumpkin wedges neatly on top, to cover the base of the pan.

Place the pan over a high heat and cook for 10 minutes or until the syrup and butter are lightly caramelized and golden. Leave to cool for 10 minutes.

Roll out the pastry 5 mm/ ¼ inch thick and cut out a 22 cm/ 9 inch diameter circle. Cover the pumpkin with the pastry, tucking it down at the edges. Brush the pastry with the beaten egg and bake for 12–15 minutes or until risen and golden (after 10 minutes, press the pastry down with a plate).

Carefully turn out on to a serving plate and pour any caramelized juices over the pumpkin. Serve hot.

CHARGRILLED POTATOES
with asparagus and porcini

275 G/10 OZ NEW POTATOES
150 G/5 OZ ASPARAGUS
150 G/5 OZ PORCINI MUSHROOMS
   (OR CHESTNUT OR STRAW
   MUSHROOMS), SLICED ABOUT
   1 CM/½ INCH THICK
6 TABLESPOONS EXTRA VIRGIN
   OLIVE OIL
3 TEASPOONS BALSAMIC VINEGAR
SEA SALT AND COARSELY GROUND
   BLACK PEPPER

SERVES 4

Cook the new potatoes in their skins in boiling salted water until just tender. Leave to cool slightly before peeling them. Cut into 1 cm/½ inch thick slices.

Preheat the grill to very hot. Brush the asparagus, mushrooms and potatoes with 4 tablespoons of the olive oil and place under the hot grill, turning them until they are golden and beginning to brown in places.

Serve immediately, drizzled with the balsamic vinegar and the remaining olive oil and sprinkled with sea salt and freshly ground black pepper.

TWICE-COOKED CHICORY

with orange and cardamom

8 HEADS OF CHICORY
   (BELGIAN ENDIVE)
85 G/3 OZ BUTTER
JUICE OF ½ LEMON
2 TEASPOONS SUGAR
SALT
JUICE AND GRATED ZEST OF
   1 ORANGE
1 TEASPOON CARDAMOM SEEDS

SERVES 4

Preheat the oven to 180°C/350°F/
Gas Mark 4.

Cut a thin slice off the bottom
of each head of chicory and
remove a little of the core, using a
small knife. Wash them carefully,
without separating the leaves.

Using 25 g/1 oz of the butter,
butter an ovenproof lidded dish
just large enough to hold all the
chicory in a single layer. Add the
chicory, 6 tablespoons water and
the lemon juice; sprinkle with half
the sugar and a little salt. Cover
with buttered greaseproof paper
and top with a plate to keep the
chicory submerged during
cooking. Cover with a lid and bake
for 30–40 minutes or until tender

when tested with the point of a
knife. Drain and set aside. This may
be prepared a day in advance.

To serve, squeeze the chicory
gently to remove excess liquid,
then dry well in a clean tea towel.
Cut them in half lengthways.

Heat the remaining butter in a
large frying pan until foaming, add
the orange zest, cardamom seeds
and the remaining sugar and cook
over a fairly high heat for 30
seconds or until lightly
caramelized. Reduce the heat, add
the halved chicory and cook
gently, turning once, until
caramelized and golden on both
sides. Pour the orange juice over
the chicory, then transfer to a
serving dish and pour over the
caramelized pan juices.

POTATO AND WALNUT GNOCCHI
with gorgonzola and basil sauce

85 G/3 OZ WALNUTS, GROUND
85 G/3 OZ GORGONZOLA CHEESE,
  CRUMBLED
325 G/12 OZ PEELED POTATOES
  (KING EDWARDS OR MARIS
  PIPER), BOILED UNTIL TENDER,
  THEN WELL MASHED, HOT
15 G/½ OZ BUTTER, SOFTENED
2 EGG YOLKS
125 G/4 OZ PLAIN FLOUR
SALT AND FRESHLY GROUND BLACK
  PEPPER

SAUCE

125 G/4 OZ BUTTER
50 G/2 OZ GORGONZOLA CHEESE,
  CRUMBLED
SMALL HANDFUL OF FRESH BASIL
  LEAVES, ROUGHLY TORN
50 G/2 OZ PARMESAN CHEESE,
  GRATED

SERVES 4

Add the ground walnuts and Gorgonzola to the hot mashed potato and beat to allow the cheese to melt. Add the butter, egg yolks, half of the flour and a little salt and pepper; mix well.

Turn the mixture on to a lightly floured surface and gently knead in the remaining flour, a little at a time, to form a smooth dough. Leave to cool.

Roll the dough into long, 2.5 cm/1 inch diameter cylinders, then cut into 2 cm/¾ inch pieces. Roll each piece over the prongs of a fork to form a decorative shape. Place the gnocchi on a floured tray and leave to dry for about 1 hour.

Poach the gnocchi, a few at a time, in plenty of boiling salted water for 2–3 minutes or until they float to the surface. Remove with a slotted spoon and keep warm.

For the sauce, place the butter in a saucepan with 3 tablespoons water, bring to the boil, then whisk in the Gorgonzola. Add the basil and season to taste. Roll the gnocchi in the sauce and serve sprinkled with the Parmesan.

BRAISED ARTICHOKES
with lemon mint pesto broth

4 GLOBE ARTICHOKES

SALT AND FRESHLY GROUND BLACK
  PEPPER

175 ML/6 FL OZ DRY WHITE WINE

6 TABLESPOONS OLIVE OIL

1 GARLIC CLOVE, CRUSHED

LEMON MINT PESTO

4 TABLESPOONS FRESH MINT LEAVES

GRATED ZEST OF ½ LEMON

1 GARLIC CLOVE, CRUSHED

4 TABLESPOONS OLIVE OIL

PINCH OF SUGAR

SERVES 4

Preheat the oven to 150°C/300°F/
Gas Mark 2. Prepare the artichokes
(page 29) and season all over with
salt and pepper.

Place the artichokes upside
down in an ovenproof dish. Whisk
the wine and oil together, stir in
the crushed garlic and pour over
the artichokes. Cover the dish with
foil or a lid, place in the oven and
braise for about 45 minutes or
until tender. Drain, reserving the
cooking liquid, and leave to cool.

For the pesto, place all the
ingredients in a liquidizer and
blend to a purée.

To serve, cut the artichokes in
half. Add the pesto to the cooking
liquid, taste and adjust the
seasoning. Pour over the artichokes
and serve at room temperature.

FRAGRANT THAI VEGETABLES
with spiced coconut

4 TABLESPOONS PEANUT OIL

50 G/2 OZ BUTTER

1 GARLIC CLOVE, CRUSHED

25 G/1 OZ FRESH GINGER, CUT
  INTO MATCHSTICKS

1 SMALL AUBERGINE, CUT INTO
  1 CM/½ INCH CUBES

1 CARROT, SLICED

150 G/5 OZ SHIITAKE MUSHROOMS

2 COURGETTES, CUT INTO 5 MM/
  ¼ INCH SLICES

4 SMALL BOK CHOY, HALVED
  LENGTHWAYS

225 G/8 OZ MANGETOUT

125 G/4 OZ CUCUMBER, HALVED,
  SEEDS REMOVED, CUT INTO
  BATONS

FRESHLY GRATED COCONUT

1 FRESH RED CHILLI, SEEDED AND
  FINELY CHOPPED

SERVES 4

Heat the peanut oil and butter in a
wok or deep-sided frying pan over
a fairly high heat. Add the garlic
and ginger and cook for 30
seconds to release the fragrance.

Add the vegetables to the pan
in the order listed and toss together
until they are cooked but retaining
their crispness.

Mix the coconut with the chilli
and sprinkle over the vegetables;
serve at once.

MY FAVOURITE GRATIN

15 G/½ OZ BUTTER

200 G/7 OZ PARSNIPS, THINLY
SLICED

SALT AND FRESHLY GROUND BLACK
PEPPER

GRATED NUTMEG

200 G/7 OZ SWEDE, THINLY SLICED

200 G/7 OZ POTATOES, THINLY
SLICED

450 ML/¾ PINT DOUBLE CREAM

150 ML/¼ PINT MILK

1 GARLIC CLOVE, CRUSHED

50 G/2 OZ CHEDDAR CHEESE,
GRATED (OPTIONAL)

SERVES 4

Preheat the oven to 180°C/350°F/
Gas Mark 4. Butter a 25 cm/
10 inch diameter (about 1.5 litre/
2 pint) gratin dish.

Arrange the parsnips in
overlapping slices in the dish and
season with salt, pepper and
nutmeg. Top with neat layers of
swede and season again, then top
with the potato slices and season
once more.

Bring the cream, milk and
garlic to the boil, then pour
through a strainer on to the
vegetables, ensuring that the liquid
covers them. (It may be necessary
to top up with more milk.)
Sprinkle over the cheese, if using,
then bake for 45–50 minutes or
until the vegetables are tender and
the top is golden and crusty.

THE BASICS

BUYING VEGETABLES

Buy fresh-looking, brightly coloured vegetables of the best quality available. They do not have to be perfectly regular in shape, but yellowing or wilted leaves or discoloured patches or sponginess are generally signs of ageing, and a hint that the vegetables will be lacking in both flavour and vitamins. If buying from a market stall, take a look behind the stall to see what the stallholder is going to put in the bag, which may be disappointingly unlike what is on display.

CHOOSING POTATOES

Some potatoes are waxy-textured; they hold their shape well and can be boiled and left whole for salads or sliced for sautéing. Others are known as 'floury'; they are easy to mash and deliciously fluffy when baked. Other varieties have a texture somewhere in between and have a number of uses in the kitchen. Here are some of the most commonly available:

VARIETY	BEST USE
Jersey Royal	Plain boiled with lashings of butter
Cyprus New	Plain boiled; salads
Desirée	Baking, frying and mashing
King Edward	All-purpose, especially mashing and frying
Maris Piper	Boiling and frying or mashing
Pentland Squire	Frying

PREPARING VEGETABLES

Vegetables such as peppers, courgettes, cucumber and aubergines should be briefly rinsed and dried, but do not usually need peeling.

Root vegetables may need washing to remove mud; peel them as thinly as possible, if at all, since the vitamins are nearest the skin.

Mushrooms should not be washed, because they are very prone to absorbing water. Wipe them with a damp cloth. Some wild mushrooms may need very careful brushing with a pastry brush to remove soil.

All vegetables should be prepared as near to the time you want to serve them as possible. Do not leave them sitting in a pan of water, as the vitamins and flavour will leach out into the water.

PREPARING ARTICHOKES

Cut the artichoke stalk 2.5 cm/1 inch below the artichoke base. Remove the fibrous, dark green outer leaves until you reach the tender, yellowish green inner leaves. Cut off one- to two-thirds from the top of the artichoke, leaving about 2.5 cm/1 inch of leaves above the base. With a small knife, trim the base and pare away the remaining tough, dark green leaves to expose the tightly packed central leaves that conceal the hairy choke. Scoop out the raw choke with a teaspoon.

BLANCHING

Blanching is a way of partly cooking vegetables in boiling water for a few seconds or minutes. Cooking is then usually stopped by holding them under cold water. The technique is used in several ways:.

- for harder vegetables that you want to cook at the same time as more tender varieties, for example in stir-frying.
- to loosen the skin of tomatoes (and also of almonds and peaches).
- to set the colour in green vegetables.

CHEF'S TIPS

- Take great care when handling chillies; they contain a chemical which can irritate the skin and will really sting if you touch your eyes, nose or mouth without washing your hands thoroughly first. You might prefer to wear rubber gloves when cutting chillies.
- Some people will always cry when chopping onions, but it is said to help if you first slice them down the middle, leaving the root end intact. It is also far easier to slice or chop them down to the roots.
- To remove onion smells, wash your hands in milk.
- Leftover garlic can be placed in a bottle and covered with olive oil to make a delicious oil for salad dressings.
- Vegetables should be cut into similar-sized pieces for even cooking and an attractive presentation. To make batons, first trim the vegetable, then cut into 4 cm/1½ inch lengths. Cut into 5 mm/¼ inch thick slices, then lay the slices flat on the work surface and cut into 5 mm/¼ inch thick sticks. Julienne strips are smaller, closer to matchstick size.

THE MASTER CHEFS

SOUPS
ARABELLA BOXER

MEZE, TAPAS AND ANTIPASTI
AGLAIA KREMEZI

PASTA SAUCES
GORDON RAMSAY

RISOTTO
MICHELE SCICOLONE

SALADS
CLARE CONNERY

MEDITERRANEAN
ANTONY WORRALL THOMPSON

VEGETABLES
PAUL GAYLER

LUNCHES
ALASTAIR LITTLE

COOKING FOR TWO
RICHARD OLNEY

FISH
RICK STEIN

CHICKEN
BRUNO LOUBET

SUPPERS
VALENTINA HARRIS

THE MAIN COURSE
ROGER VERGÉ

ROASTS
JANEEN SARLIN

WILD FOOD
ROWLEY LEIGH

PACIFIC
JILL DUPLEIX

CURRIES
PAT CHAPMAN

HOT AND SPICY
PAUL AND JEANNE RANKIN

THAI
JACKI PASSMORE

CHINESE
YAN-KIT SO

VEGETARIAN
KAREN LEE

DESSERTS
MICHEL ROUX

CAKES
CAROLE WALTER

COOKIES
ELINOR KLIVANS

THE MASTER CHEFS

Text © copyright 1996 Paul Gayler

Paul Gayler has asserted his right to be
identified as the Author of this Work.

Photographs © copyright 1996 Simon Wheeler

First published in 1996 by
WEIDENFELD & NICOLSON
THE ORION PUBLISHING GROUP
ORION HOUSE
5 UPPER ST MARTIN'S LANE
LONDON WC2H 9EA

British Library Cataloguing-in-Publication data
A catalogue record for this book is available
from the British Library.

ISBN 0 297 83635 8

DESIGNED BY THE SENATE
EDITOR MAGGIE RAMSAY
FOOD STYLIST JOY DAVIES
ASSISTANT KATY HOLDER